ABIDE

Holding Out Under God's Grace

Letitia Evans

Published by Light House Media Publishing
P.O. Box 2567, Elizabeth City, NC 27901
Web: www.letitiaevans.com
Email: letitia@letitiaevans.com

Printed U.S.A.

Front & Back Cover Designs by Lighthouse Media
Publishing

Abide: Holding Out Under God's Grace

ISBN: 978-1-60141-643-8

ROOTED AND OVERFLOWING MINISTRY

Roots Grow Deep Series

CONTENTS

Introduction

Rooted and Overflowing Ministries is committed to inspiring women to become confident and resilient in the faith. The work we do is supported by Colossians 2:6-7, which says

> *"Therefore as you have received Christ Jesus the Lord, so walk in Him, having been firmly rooted and now being built up in Him and established in your faith, just as you were instructed and overflowing with* gratitude."

Our Mission

Our mission is to help women gain confidence and resilience in the Christian faith through studying the Bible and cultivating a life of prayer and devotion to God.

Our mission is driven by the charge to reach the lost with the message of salvation through Jesus Christ and to equip believers for Christian life and service.

We accomplish our mission by building community and developing content and merchandise designed to supplement the Christian woman's faith walk. We accomplish this through podcasts, blogs, event hosting, and other ministry endeavors.

In this Publication

The bible tells us that the one who endures to the end shall be saved. It also admonishes us to endure hardness as good soldiers. How can this be achieved when trials, tests, and temptations confront the Chrisian daily?

It can be done through abiding in Christ. As Christians abide in Christ continually, they are able to hold up through hard times under God's grace. In this book, be encouraged to be steadfast and unmovable, always abounding in Christ.

-Chapter 1-

Abide

Let's explore what it means to abide with the Lord. When we decide to devote ourselves to Christ, it takes effort on our part.

"Abide in me, and I in you. As the branch cannot bear fruit of itself, except it abide in the vine; no more can ye, except ye abide in me. I am the vine, ye are the branches: He that abideth in me, and I in him, the same bringeth forth much fruit: for without me ye can do nothing." John 15:4-5

This month I'm kicking off a series of blog entries entitled "A Devoted Life."

Throughout this month and sprinkled through the year, this will be a place to unpack scriptures that encourage a life that is devoted to God, through Jesus Christ.

Over time the idea of devotions and setting aside time for personal devotion activities like (but not limited to) prayer and scripture reading, has gotten away from the church.

Without getting into speculation as to why we've gotten away from it, this is a great time to reacquaint ourselves with the practice of setting ourselves, our minds, and our attention on Christ.

To get us started, let's explore what it means to abide in Jesus Christ. When we make the decision to devote ourselves to Christ, it takes effort on our part. It requires us to be deliberate in setting ourselves apart for and to Jesus Christ.

Equipped to Abide

Within the verses of John chapter 15 are three temptations that Jesus was equipping the disciples to overcome in order to abide in Him:

1) The temptation to reject the teachings that did not reveal Christ as Savior,

2) The temptation to grow strange toward each other, which is to not show fellowship or love.

And also,

3) The temptation to shrink back from their responsibilities as apostles when times got hard. Each of these instances can likely ring true in our personal lives.

And now, just like then, Jesus' words are meant to give us strength, confidence, and power to live a holy life in a fallen world AND bear fruit while doing it. Of course, this ability is not something we accomplish on our own.

Equipped to Unyielding Faith

In verse 4, we see where Jesus says "abide in me." The Merriam-Webster definition of "abide" is to endure without yielding or giving up, to accept without objection, and to remain stable or fixed in a state.

When you look at a vine you see that it grows from the root and grips its foundation and then there are many, many branches that come from it and they wind, climb, and coil within themselves and other branches.

On the branches you'll find either

flowers like the morning glory, fruit like grapes, or vegetables like the cucumber. When you break a branch from off of the vine, it dries up. The branch does not have the necessary nutrients to live. It's just all by itself, subject to being blown away or picked up and thrown away or even burned up, as it's illustrated within chapter 15.

But when the branches are connected to the vine it continues to grow and flourish. It gets nutrients from the root and yields its crop. People can pick the crop and because the branch is still connected to the vine, more will grow. This illustrates the value of being connected to Christ in order to remain strong.

When we help people, do our jobs, do our schoolwork, and do it all in our own strength, we get burned out, frustrated, confused, and out of sorts.

All kinds of ugly just sets in because we tried to do something and Jesus already said we can do nothing unless we're abiding in Him.

When we abide in Jesus Christ, the true vine, we will always have what we need to bear fruit. Fruit is the evidence of and benefits for being connected to Jesus Christ.

The fruit we can display includes transformed personalities, Godly temperament, honest and moral conversations, good works, the display of being devoted to God in prayer and reading His Word and being in His presence.

We cannot do these things on our own or according to our own righteousness. We need Jesus to survive and thrive in this life. I encourage you today to connect or reconnect with Christ and stay connected...Abide in Christ.

Notes:

____

____

____

____

____

____

____

____

-Chapter 2-

Holding Out Under God's Grace

Take heart. What was designed to take you out will ultimately make you stronger.

"Each time he said, "My grace is all you need. My power works best in weakness." So now I am glad to boast about my weaknesses, so that the power of Christ can work through me. That's why I take pleasure in my weaknesses, and in the insults, hardships, persecutions, and troubles that I suffer for Christ. For when I am weak, then I am strong." 2 Corinthians 12:9-10

Take Heart in Faith

What was designed to take you out will ultimately make you stronger. Trust how God is bringing you through what you're going through. (Go ahead and read that again.) God could change things for you in an instant. But if He isn't working it out that way, be content with knowing that He's got a reason and it is good.

God's got a reason for taking His time and making you feel every single bump and scrape along this leg of your journey. God's way of pruning us can seem unfair, tedious, inconvenient, and harsh. You might even think your pruning time should be over by now. Yet, here you are...here WE are: battle worn, bruised, embarrassed, vulnerable, shaken– and bothered about it.

Take Comfort in God

God gets it. He knows it's not an easy road. He also knows it's the best road for us because it will lead us to the blessed destination that He has reserved for us. God sees what we can't see. He knows what He has to work out of us so that He can work in us and through us.

And He knows how long it will take. There's an choir song lyric that says "Lord, help me to hold out...until my change has come." This is a fitting prayer set to a melody that we can have in our hearts as we call on God to help us hold out until our current trial is over.

Notes:

____

____

____

____

____

____

____

____

____

____

____

-Chapter 3-

A Clean Heart

Whether it's the end of the year or the beginning of the new year, while the pace is a little slower, take this time to sit before the Lord with Psalm 51.

My Story

As a young girl, growing up in Dayton, Ohio, God favored me to attend Bethel Missionary Baptist Church, under the leadership of Dr. Charles S. Brown and his lovely wife Mrs. Joan S. Brown.

I have many beautiful memories at Bethel. Memories that I cherish to this very day. From time to time I will share them here, along with wonderful memories I made while attending Mt. Calvary Baptist Church and even now at Mt. Zion Church of God in Christ in North Carolina.

Bethel was known for singing soaring anthems, peaceful chants, and contemplative hymns, all with a splash of gospel flavor. Among them is a song composed by Margaret J. Douroux, PhD, entitled "Give Me a Clean Heart." You can learn more about Dr. Douroux, this song, and her tremendous contributions to sacred music by clicking here.

The smoothest and richest alto voice in the choir at Bethel when I was about 10 years old was from the person of Sis. Wanda Bryant. I cannot hear in my mind another voice leading the chorus and singing the verses to "Give Me a Clean Heart."

The verses from this song highlight verses from Psalm 51 and stands among countless compositions that beckon us set ourselves before the Lord in prayer with a request for Him to do what only He can do to purify our hearts and help us persevere in serving Him.

Before I go on, I'll share a summary of why Psalm 51 was written. This psalm is one of lament and was composed by King David. After David's unlawful encounter with Bathsheba and after murdering her husband to cover it all up,

Nathan the prophet confronted David about it. You can read about it from the Bible here. David came to grips with the error of his ways and repented. Thus, we have Psalm 51.

My Psalm

During fall and the end of the year, these times bring a time of retrospection for most people. We celebrate and are thankful for what went well. We also think about what did not go well and what we want to   do to make sure we have a better year. For a person of faith, this retrospection includes our walk with God.

Our lives are affected by many outside variables. Changes in our health, work, relationships, unfulfilled dreams, money concerns, general overwhelm, grief, and more can move us out of step with God.

We daily run the risk of becoming cynical to the point where we no longer trust God deeply. We only trust Him in theory. We trust Him on the surface so that we can save Christian face with ourselves and others who know we serve and (gasp!) lead in ministry.

My Encouragement

Whether it's the end of the year or the beginning of the new year, while the pace is a little slower, take this time to sit before the Lord with Psalm 51.

It is one of many psalms of lament in the Bible, but somehow over time this one has stood out when we find ourselves needing to seek God's forgiveness and cleansing from sinful thoughts, deeds, and motivations.

Many of us are not enjoying this life that God has blessed us with because we just haven't come clean with Him. We haven't stopped to take stock of our individual life's direction. We're just going through the motions hoping God is pleased with us.

When God cleanses our hearts and minds, we get renewed joy, peace, vision, wisdom, stability, and strength to live our best lives and enjoy what God has blessed us with while we serve Him.

The Lord knows how to search our hearts for what displeases Him and doesn't serve us well. Let us let King David's script be our guide in prayer as we enter the new year (the new decade!) and let the Holy Spirit do the work while we trust God and live.

Notes:

____

____

____

____

____

____

____

____

About the Author

Letitia Evans has dedicated her life to inspiring people to achieve their God-given potential. Letitia's passion for faith and resilience shines brightly through her work and ministry.

Letitia hosts the podcast "Rooted and Overflowing," where she and her guests share thoughtful reflections and explore the depths of faith and the joys of gratitude. You can find her podcast at rootedandoverflowing.com.